Read With Carylee Publishing books may be ordered through booksellers or by contacting:

Read With Carylee Publishing
PO Box 937
Bristow, VA 20136
www.rwcpublishing.com

ISBN: 979-8-218-47135-4 (sc)
ISBN: 979-8-218-47134-7 (e)

Read With Carylee Publishing 10/8/2024

Read With Carylee
PUBLISHING

Dedicated to the matriarchs of the family. Who continue to show love in everything you do to keep our families together.

Trey woke up Thanksgiving morning. He was glad to be able to sleep later because of the holiday. He could hear that his parents were already up and bustling about. But why? It was a holiday and they didn't need to go to work. Why were they up so early?

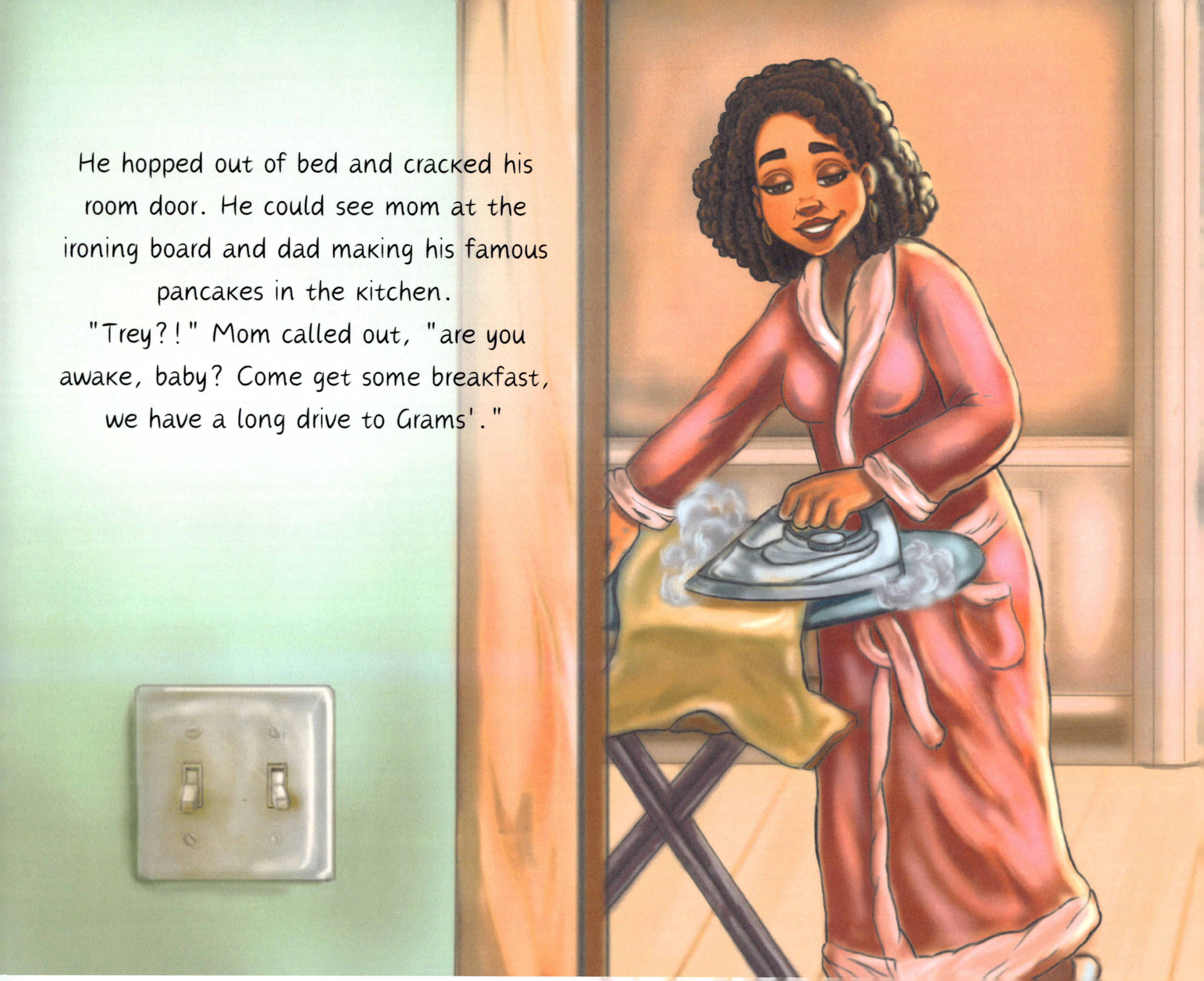

He hopped out of bed and cracked his room door. He could see mom at the ironing board and dad making his famous pancakes in the kitchen.

"Trey?!" Mom called out, "are you awake, baby? Come get some breakfast, we have a long drive to Grams'."

Trey stepped out of his room, still
wiping the sleep out of his eyes.
His older sister Brittany, rushed by him,
almost knocking him out of the way.
"Hey!" Trey yelled, "Watch it!"

"You snooze, you lose, little bro," Brittany exclaimed, sticking her tongue out at Trey. She is 10 years old and wanted to be the first to get dad's pancakes.

"Come on kids, you know there's more than enough for everyone." Dad said, reassuring Trey.

"Baby, go wash up and come eat." Mom chimed in.

Trey washed up for breakfast and joined the rest of the family at the kitchen table. There were pancakes, scrambled eggs, bacon, breakfast sausage, hash browns, fruit and 2 kinds of juices. It was Thanksgiving alright, the day meant for eating.

Dad blessed the food and they all got to eating.

"Dad, how come your pancakes are soooo good? They're even better than when we go to a restaurant." Brittany asked.

"Cause it's my Gram, your great-Gram's recipe," Dad started before taking a bite, "and it also has an extra dash of love."

"Love?" Trey asked, scratching his head.

"Yes, Trey. That's how you get the soul in soul food. With that extra dash of love." Mom answered. Trey was still puzzled. He wondered where in the cupboard was the "love". He is 6 and knows how to read. He doesn't remember ever seeing a jar of "love" in the cupboard.

After breakfast it was time to get ready to go. He was a little annoyed that he had to wear his Sunday clothes. It was Thursday. But Mom said they had to look their best.

As they got in the family SUV, he saw gifts and packages in the back. Placed securely in the seat next to his, was mom's famous carrot cake. One of two that she made the night before.

"Okay, I think we're ready to go. I can't wait to get to Gram's for dinner." Dad said. "And to see the rest of the family of course," he followed up, with a cheesy smile. Mom laughed at him.

Trey began to wonder, what is so special about going to Gram's for dinner. Did she own a restaurant?

"Now kids, be sure to let us know if you need to use the bathroom. It'll be about 3 hours till we get to Gram's." Mom announced.

3 hours?! Trey thought. His eyes widened and he took a deep breath. His mind was racing. Why on earth would we drive 3 hours for dinner? This must be some really good food.

Dad turned on the engine and they were off. Over a few rivers, through winding roads and woods.

The view out the window was even better than the smartpad screen meant to keep Trey busy.

He loved taking in the sights, especially going over the bridges.

Trey went through 2 cities with many tall buildings and finally they turned into a gated yard with a bumpy driveway. Then finally, they were at Gram's house.

As soon as Dad opened the door of the house, you could hear the roar of people talking and laughing. They were pulled in by hugs and high-fives. Everyone was happy to see them. "Hey Big Trey!" A man greeted Trey's father. The house was warm and the smells were inviting. Whatever was cooking, it sure smells good.

All the women greeted Trey with smiles. There were a lot of, "Hi Baby, remember me?" and "Oh look how handsome you've gotten." These were aunts and older cousins. The men were more cool, with their, "What's up buddy?" and "Putter there lil fella." Which was either a high-five or a low-five. Some even gave a side hand slap, with a slide, a grip at the fingers, and a sort of snap when they pulled away. They call that daps. Trey had seen his father do it many times with his friends, but he hadn't mastered it yet.

There were so many people to see. As everyone got settled, Trey followed his dad down to the basement. There were card games and domino games being played at a few folding tables and over at the far end, was a group of men watching football. Trey spotted his grandfather "Pop-pop" and ran over jumping up on him in his lazy chair.

"Hey, gotta be careful, Trey. Can't be jumping too hard on Pop-pop's old bones." Dad laughed.

"I'll show you old bones," Pop-pop replied, as they did a little shadow boxing, before bringing it in for a hug. "Good to see you, son."

"You too, Dad."

Trey stayed a while watching football with Dad, Pop-pop and 3 other men who were his uncle and cousins, but the smells from upstairs were calling him.

Trey snuck away and wandered into the dining room. There was a long table with more food than he had ever seen. He went along counting chairs and seeing all the food that was placed in the center of this long table. There were 24 chairs. There had to be a lot of food to feed all those people.

There was turkey, ham, baked chicken, fried chicken, yams, potatoes, fried green tomatoes, corn on the cob, cornbread, and a couple casseroles that were covered. Green beans, pasta salad, green salad. You name it, it was probably on the table. Over at the end of the table, was another table with dessert. There was Mom's famous carrot cake, there was cherry pie, sweet potato pie, and 3 chocolate cakes.

"Hi Baby!" Mom called out from the kitchen. She was there with Brittany, aunt Millie, aunt Jessica, aunt Alexis, cousins Riley, Calie, Tiffany, and Tiana. Grandma Joanne was busy at the stove and the family Matriarch Gram Shirley was putting food into containers.

Trey went into the kitchen and gave Gram the biggest hug. He asked, "Gram Shirley, did you make ALL of this?"

"Well, I had help from these ladies here, baby. But I'm thankful that we can all come together for this Thanksgiving and I can cook for all my babies." Gram Shirley answered. "Sing him your song, Gram." Brittany blurted with a giggle. "Oh, I was just being silly, baby. But ok." Gram held Trey's hand and walked over to the dining room. "Look!" She said pointing to the table filled with food.

We got corn, we got beans,
We got tomatoes, potatoes,
Ham and greens,
We got chicken and turkey
Made just for our family
And that's a happy thanksgiving
Yes that's a happy thanksgiving

Everyone in the kitchen was clapping and dancing. Trey even joined in. Laughter filled the kitchen and dining room. And finally, it was time to eat.

"I think we're ready." Gram said, still laughing. "Trey, why don't you go down and tell everyone that dinner is ready."

Trey scurried off, giddy with excitement. He couldn't wait to give everything on the table a taste.

Everyone came together at this great big table. Trey's mouth was watering; he was ready to dig in. The entire room grew quiet as Gram Shirley stood at the head of the table.

"Family," she began, "I am so grateful to have everyone here at this Thanksgiving table. We have much to be thankful for." There were nods, yes', mmhmms, and Amens of agreement from all around the table. We all bowed our heads as Gram Shirley prayed.

There was so much food. Trey wanted to have a little bit of everything. When Gram Shirley was done praying, Pop-pop clapped and rubbed his hands together and said, "Alright everybody. Let's eat!"

Food was passed all around the table. Trey got mashed potatoes, Mac and Cheese, Turkey, Stuffing, Cornbread. Mom made him add greens and salad. There was just so much, but with just that, he was stuffed.

The doorbell rang and everyone stopped. Did we forget someone before we started eating?

Dad and Uncle Steve grabbed some food containers that were in the kitchen and headed to the front door. "Mom, where are they going with all that food?" I asked.

"Well," Mom began, "Gram didn't only cook for us. She also cooks for those who may not be able to visit their families for Thanksgiving."

"Wow! Gram is awesome."

"Yes she is!" Mom agreed.

Trey was so full, he wasn't ready for dessert just yet. Gram was still sitting and talking, while the other family members helped clear the table. He went over to Gram and gave her a big hug. "Gram, thank you. This was the best Thanksgiving ever."

"Aww, you're welcome baby. What was your favorite part?" She asked.

His eyes opened wide, "All the food. There was so much. And Mom said that you give to other people who don't have their family with them for Thanksgiving."

"Oh yes!" Gram Shirley answered, "It is always better to give than to receive. God has blessed us with plenty, so we should always be happy to share with others. And that is really what Thanksgiving is all about."

"Oh and I love your song. Can we sing it again?" Trey asked.

"Of course, baby. As long as you help me." Answered Gram.

The whole family gathered around singing, clapping, and dancing to Gram's Thanksgiving song.

The Family Thanksgiving Song

Verse 1
We all come for one day
Different towns, different states
Show our love, eat and pray
On this Thanksgiving Day
Our family's come together
Traveled all sorts of weather
In cars, planes, buses and trains
We have come to enjoy this day

Chorus
We got corn, we got beans,
We got tomatoes, potatoes,
Ham and greens,
We got chicken and turkey
Made just for our family
And that's a happy thanksgiving
Yes that's a happy thanksgiving

Verse 2
I love having you all here
This is my favorite time of the year
My love's the main
Ingredient in every dish
I do it all for you
And love every moment
I'll just ask you this one thing
Please sing this anthem
Every year with cheer
In your cars, planes, buses and trains
Shout it loud on this special day

Chorus
(Repeat)

And that's a happy thanksgiving
Yes that's a happy thanksgiving
That's a happy thanksgiving, family!

The Family Thanksgiving Song

Listen Now

Printed in the USA
CPSIA information can be obtained
at www.ICGtesting.com
LVRC101115181124
796716LV00013B/201

9798218471354